UAE BUSINESS ESSENTIALS

Practical Legal Protections for Individuals, Entrepreneurs and SMEs

KAMAL K. JABBAR

Media Regulatory Office Application Number MC-01-01-2040541
Age Classification: E

تم تصنيف محتوى هذا الكتاب ضمن الفئة العامة التي تُلائم محتوى
ة القثلةواشبلراباوفاظنل اقم انصتيلـف العمري الصادر عنـ

Printed by Water Dance Printing.
PO Box 25151 Dubai, UAE.
Email: water.dance.print@icloud.com

PRAISE FOR "UAE Business Essentials"

"..refreshing insights and a very useful guide...the ideas put forward in this manual will be valuable for entrepreneurs who either aspire to do business in the UAE or find themselves in tight spots while navigating the country's complex business milieu. A more academic approach to the subject would have turned this brief yet rewarding book into an inaccessible text. The author ought to be commended for giving preference to simplicity without compromising on research."

South Asia Magazine
(southasia.com.pk)

"A brilliant book which covers a variety of important topics from incorporating your company to compliance in E-Commerce. A fast read, cleverly written with references that range from Stoic philosophy to quotes from Hedge fund managers. An essential read for anyone looking to traverse through the complex legal playing field of UAE."

Ahmed Nasir Warraich,
Director, Scotiabank

"With zippy prose, interesting anecdotes, and amusing quotes, this book is essential reading for those navigating the UAE business / legal landscape. 5 Stars!"

- **Faisal Fazli,**
Director, Citibank

"…very valuable, useful information, making it easy for a new entrant to the UAE…"

Surender Singh Kandhari,
Chairman and founder, Al Dobowi Group

"Crisply written, fluid tone..."

Profit Magazine
(profit.pakistantoday.com.pk)

"In brief, if you are looking to operate a SME in the UAE, I highly recommend this. There is something in this book the knowledge of which will pay for the book a hundred times over. What is that something? That depends on your business and how it goes, but ultimately, there's such a lot of clearly critical information here that something within its pages will allow you to avoid a costly misstep."

Anastasia Styles

"I found this book to be not only enlightening but also very practical and accessible. A must read for anyone who is wanting to enter into the corporate community in the UAE or those who are already well established in the same!"

Riddhi Sandil, Ph.D.

"Correctly positioned as a 'no-nonsense' business guide, the book addresses aspiring entrepreneurs, new or existing investors as well as individuals seeking employment and provides all the essentials that constitute sound practical business advice. Easy to understand and refer to, this book is a composite of facts, short anecdotes, tips and actionable insights that will help readers spot opportunities, avoid mistakes, make informed decisions and be better equipped to handle setbacks. The book is conversational in tone and provides the right amount of information to guide readers through the initial phases of business, what to look out for in contracts, common pitfalls and ways to avoid them."

Aurora Magazine (aurora.dawn.com)

"Clear, concise and easy to read...great writing style, using relevant examples...a book I definitely want to keep handy at all times!"

**Amna Zafar,
Real Estate Investor**

"Concise, clear...easy to read and loaded with useful insights…"

W. Drake

"..remarkably well-written with incredible strategies, information and actionable tactics.."

Evelyn P.

"a very well written book of insight and inspiration for anyone looking for more information on how to succeed and prosper in any financial endeavor, especially related to business dealings within the UAE."

Catherine Grainger

"I fall under the category of someone interested in working with a business based in the UAE. This book has a rich abundance of information, from an early history lesson about the UAE, to explaining (to my surprise) about the different legal system and business rules in each area. Very helpful and informative."

Jan Hart

"A must have reference for lawyers working in UAE or anyone interested in the UAE's legal / commercial landscape."

Layla El Wafi

UAE BUSINESS ESSENTIALS

**Practical Legal Protections for
Individuals, Entrepreneurs and SMEs**

Kamal K. Jabbar

UAE BUSINESS ESSENTIALS

Copyright © 2021 Kamal K. Jabbar

www.kamaljabbar.com

All rights reserved. No portion of this book may be reproduced in any form without permission from the publisher, except as permitted by U.S. copyright law.

For permissions contact: info@kamaljabbar.com

Although this publication is designed to provide accurate information in regard to the subject matter covered, the publisher and the author assume no responsibility for errors, inaccuracies, omissions, or any other inconsistencies herein. This publication is meant as a source of valuable information for the reader, however it is not meant as a replacement for direct expert assistance.

For Zaka,

who arrived with drama one hot August morning

and changed our lives forever

CHAPTER 1

Prologue

When I arrived on the shores of Dubai many moons ago searching for hidden bullion, I remember meeting a chirpy Australian lawyer at a business networking event. He was a 5-year PQE, University of Sydney-educated solicitor and he, like me, had just moved to the city.

We got chatting about our experiences.

When he sputtered something about *"gharrar"*, the Sharia principle of uncertainty that has the capacity to vitiate a contract, I was impressed. The boy had done his homework.

"Actually, I'm quite at sea, mate," he said, looking into the distance after I had expressed appreciation of his knowledge of an age-old, Islamic legal principle.

The statement sounded like a confession.

But I knew what he meant: entrepreneurs (and lawyers) from common law jurisdictions such as America, England, Pakistan, India, New Zealand and Australia can often feel rudderless when thrust into the complex civil law systems in the Middle East.

In common law countries, judges interpret the laws created by legislators and play an active role in shaping them. For example, they can be expected to rely on earlier court judgments and apply them to individual cases with similar fact patterns and questions of law. In some countries, courts can even strike down laws they deem unconstitutional.

The nuances of doing business and the cogs of the judicial machinery in civil law systems are very different.

In civil law systems, the emphasis is on applying written, codified law rather than on precedent. The role of the judge is more circumscribed: establishing the facts and applying the statute. France, Germany and Brazil are examples of civil law systems.

The UAE is an interesting amalgam - and far from being monolithically common law or civil law based.

It is a civil law jurisdiction with over 50 "free zones". These free zones have the right to make their own rules.

Two of these free zones have their own common law based legal systems in which most of the federal laws of the UAE do not apply.

Court documents and proceedings in the local courts are in Arabic. There is no concept of binding precedent, no established system of publishing judgments and business is often conducted with local nuances unfamiliar to the uninitiated.

It is an ecosystem that can sometimes mystify laymen as well as lawyers.

This book is a no-nonsense guide to help you understand UAE's business environment.

It will enable you to have more productive and informed conversations with your advisers and protect yourself legally so you can thrive in one of the most vibrant and diverse economies in the world.

Who am I?

The attorney tells the accused, "I have some good news and some bad news."

"What's the bad news?" asks the accused.

"The bad news is, your blood is all over the crime scene, and the DNA tests prove you did it."

"What's the good news?"

"Your cholesterol is 130."

I'm not sure whether it was the high school debate team, lawyer jokes, the TV series *Matlock* or an irrepressible passion for justice but the commitment to becoming a lawyer got chiselled in early in life.

When my partner and I went it alone and set up our firm, many of the initial days were spent tapping our fingers on our desks, waiting for the phone to ring.

Setting up your own enterprise can be daunting.

There was excitement mixed with trepidation.

We had leapt out of a plane flashing victory signs. But there were days when I would look back to check if I had packed a parachute.

From a time when my first client could only pay me with a jar of pickles to advising on transactions involving Fortune 500 companies, it has been quite a plane ride.

Over the years, whilst in private practice and in-house roles, I have worked with individuals and SMEs, large regional corporates such as Al-Futtaim, Landmark Group and Olayan Group and global mega-caps such as Amazon, Shell and Schlumberger.

Working with a British emerging markets financial institution with a presence in over 70 countries gives you a little flavour of doing things in different parts of the world. The cutting of red tape in Cote d' Ivoire or rising business costs in Singapore reminds us of how we all are connected elements on the same canvas.

Dubai, a truly international city, has been home for the last decade.

Along the way, I have learned a few things - and forgotten others.

I have learnt that every large company was once a small business requiring quality legal advice to navigate the challenges of growth.

These pages contain distilled guidance on the UAE's business environment that will help you protect yourself and your business.

CONTENTS

Chapter 1 Prologue 5

Chapter 2 From Trucial States to Towers in the Sky 13

Chapter 3 Start Right 19

Chapter 4 Secret Sauce - Using NDAs 22

Chapter 5 Protect Your Chips 28

Chapter 6 Safeguard your IP 48

Chapter 7 The Benjamins - Raising Funds While Remaining Protected 55

Chapter 8 Giving Security 62

Chapter 9 Employment & HR 66

Chapter 10 E-commerce 74

Chapter 11 Consumer Protection 78

Chapter 12 Time to turn off the lights? 80

Epilogue 86

Before you go 87

Acknowledgments 89

Also by the author

Fiction

Selling Oranges in a Banana Republic (1996)

Defunct (1993)

UAE BUSINESS ESSENTIALS

Practical Legal Protections for
Individuals, Entrepreneurs and SMEs

Kamal K. Jabbar

UAE BUSINESS ESSENTIALS

Copyright © 2021 Kamal K. Jabbar

www.kamaljabbar.com

All rights reserved. No portion of this book may be reproduced in any form without permission from the publisher, except as permitted by U.S. copyright law.

For permissions contact: info@kamaljabbar.com

Although this publication is designed to provide accurate information in regard to the subject matter covered, the publisher and the author assume no responsibility for errors, inaccuracies, omissions, or any other inconsistencies herein. This publication is meant as a source of valuable information for the reader, however it is not meant as a replacement for direct expert assistance.

Two of these free zones have their own common law based legal systems in which most of the federal laws of the UAE do not apply.

Court documents and proceedings in the local courts are in Arabic. There is no concept of binding precedent, no established system of publishing judgments and business is often conducted with local nuances unfamiliar to the uninitiated.

It is an ecosystem that can sometimes mystify laymen as well as lawyers.

This book is a no-nonsense guide to help you understand UAE's business environment.

It will enable you to have more productive and informed conversations with your advisers and protect yourself legally so you can thrive in one of the most vibrant and diverse economies in the world.

But I knew what he meant: entrepreneurs (and lawyers) from common law jurisdictions such as America, England, Pakistan, India, New Zealand and Australia can often feel rudderless when thrust into the complex civil law systems in the Middle East.

In common law countries, judges interpret the laws created by legislators and play an active role in shaping them. For example, they can be expected to rely on earlier court judgments and apply them to individual cases with similar fact patterns and questions of law. In some countries, courts can even strike down laws they deem unconstitutional.

The nuances of doing business and the cogs of the judicial machinery in civil law systems are very different.

In civil law systems, the emphasis is on applying written, codified law rather than on precedent. The role of the judge is more circumscribed: establishing the facts and applying the statute. France, Germany and Brazil are examples of civil law systems.

The UAE is an interesting amalgam - and far from being monolithically common law or civil law based.

It is a civil law jurisdiction with over 50 "free zones". These free zones have the right to make their own rules.

It is not an academic paper, a legal textbook nor is it exhaustive on the topics it covers.

It is a short, succinct overview of vast, complex subjects.

By reading it, you can better understand the legal systems (yes, there are more than one) in the UAE.

This book will provide you with the essential elements of how to structure your business, protect your hard-earned money and assets while you work on making your venture outstanding.

Getting to know the lay of the land is the first step, so let's move on!

Is this book for you?

Thanks for picking up a copy of this book.

Let's start with a quick check on whether you're in the right place.

This book is for you if you:

- wish to know more about UAE's business environment and legal system
- are an entrepreneur planning to launch a business in the UAE
- are running a small or medium-sized business
- are seeking guidance on protecting yourself and your assets
- are investing or looking to invest in the UAE
- wish to have more informed conversations with your advisers
- are employed by or do business with a UAE based company

It will take you through the initial phases of your business, what to look out for in your contracts, show you common pitfalls and how to avoid them.

This book is not intended as or a substitute for legal advice.

Your Free Gift

As a thank-you for your purchase, I am offering a free bonus: a two-page book summary in the form of a downloadable PDF file that summarizes the contents of this book for you on a couple of pages.

It contains a relevant table and a checklist.

You can save it or print it out as a handy reminder and reference guide.

Download your bonus at:

www.kamaljabbar.com/book

2

From Trucial States to Towers in the Sky

A spoonful of recent history...

Let's take a quick look in the rear-view mirror to see what happened before the skyscrapers went up and the UAE sent a mission to Mars.

The seven emirates that comprise present-day UAE were known as the Trucial Coast or the Trucial States, an informal British protectorate. Treaties or truces with the Brits between 1820 and 1892 safeguarded British trading routes while offering the sheikhs protection against the territorial ambitions of regional forces.

On 2nd December 1971, with all treaties revoked the previous day, the six sheikhdoms (or "Emirates") of Dubai, Abu Dhabi, Sharjah, Ajman, Umm Al Quwain and Fujairah formed the United Arab Emirates. Ras Al Khaima joined the federation in February the following year.

A federal constitution was put in place. The federal government retained exclusive jurisdiction in substantive matters such as foreign policy, national security and defence. Under Article 122 of the Constitution, the governments of the Emirates could legislate on all matters not expressly reserved for the Federal Government.

Federal law would always trump local law and the law of the land continues to be derived from the following sources:

- The UAE Federal Constitution;
- Federal laws and regulations;
- Laws and regulations of individual Emirates;
- Shari'ah principles; and
- Free Zone regulations (as applicable).

The Role of Shariah

The UAE prides itself as a modern, progressive and ambitious country.

With over 10 million tourists visiting each year, Dubai is among the most sought-after cities on the tourist map. Some of the world's biggest names in music perform at its nightclubs, bars and beaches.

It is flamboyant, stylish and oozes urban panache.

So what role does Shariah play?

While the UAE federal constitution provides for Shariah being the main source of law in the UAE, it's generally only applied as an interpretative tool - and only to issues where a statute is silent. It is used in religious and personal law matters and transactions where shariah compliance is expressly required.

Riba, or interest, which is forbidden under shariah, for example, is generally enforceable in conventional financing transactions.

The UAE also prides itself on being a tolerant and multicultural society and one of the only countries with a government ministry dedicated explicitly to tolerance.

It is a civil law jurisdiction and legislation is mix of Islamic and European concepts of civil law similar to the Egyptian legal code.

Free Zones

Within the UAE, there are over 50 "free zones". These free zones have the right to make their own rules.

A couple of the free zones, Abu Dhabi Global Markets (ADGM) and the Dubai International Financial Centre (DIFC), are common law jurisdictions and have their own court systems. Other than criminal and family laws, the laws of the UAE do not apply to these financial free zones.

Proceedings in the DIFC and ADGM courts are in English. Retired judges from common law jurisdictions generally adjudicate cases; their judgments are published and are binding.

The ADGM has rules in place (Application of English Law Regulation 2015) that make English common law directly applicable in its courts together with a wide range of statutes.

The DIFC and ADGM courts differ greatly from onshore courts where the proceedings are in Arabic.

Mainland

Onshore, on mainland UAE, the judicial system varies from emirate to emirate.

Five of the seven emirates submit to a federal system.

Dubai and Ras Al Khaimah opted out of the federal structure and retained their own court systems.

Abu Dhabi is unlike any other emirate because it has a parallel system of federal and local courts.

Dubai's courts comprise a Court of First Instance, a Court of Appeal, and a Court of Cassation.

Like most of the Middle East, Emirati citizens are spared the ordeal of jury duty, with all cases being decided by either a single judge or a panel of three judges.

The country is pro-business and encourages innovation and investment.

Startups and SMEs make up over 90% of the businesses in the UAE.

3

Start Right

You go out for drinks and dinner to the DIFC with your friend, Sara.

She's a smart girl, reads the Financial Times, and her consulting background makes her a sensible choice to discuss the company you plan to launch. So, over multiple glasses of Malbec going late into the night, you discuss your business model and your revolutionary product.

As expected, Sara provides interesting, actionable insights.

"She's the kind of senior management I will need to make this a success," you say to yourself. "Doubt she would consider leaving her blue-chip career for a risk-laden startup, though," you think when the evening ends.

You spend the next six months structuring the company, developing and then finally launching the product, which gets prominent coverage in the media.

The following day, Sara calls to congratulate you. She says that she has been made redundant from her job and wants to assert her equity share in the company and join full time.

"Equity share?" you think while falling back from your chair.

Sara hearkens back to that bibulous night in the DIFC when she provided you with the guidance, information and knowledge upon which your recently launched product is now based. She discussed the idea with others in the industry and they too feel it has huge growth potential. They are even ready to partner with her on it.

She has the right to 50% of your company, she says and adds, as though you had forgotten, that her fiancée is a lawyer.

As absurd as you may consider this, if you don't settle with her, Sara could take legal action against your company and slow down your financing efforts.

And unlike mainland courts which generally only award monetary damages, DIFC courts regularly issue injunctions (stay orders).

Newly formed companies and startups are risky and any new business mired in litigation is a turn-off for investors.

This is where IP protections, non-disclosure agreements, and other elements of 'starting right' come in.

We'll come to IP but let's deal with NDAs first…

4

Secret Sauce

Using NDAs

What do Krispy Kreme Doughnuts, KFC and the New York Times Best-Seller List have in common?

They all have closely guarded trade secrets known only to a few individuals who are tightly bound by confidentiality agreements.

The recipe for Krispy Kreme Doughnuts lies in a vault in its corporate headquarters in North Carolina.

Colonel Harland Sanders initially kept his secret chicken recipe in his head but eventually wrote it down. Despite having stores and franchises worldwide, only a few select employees bound by strict confidentiality agreements know it.

Two companies blend portions of the mixture and then run through a computer processing system for standardisation as an added layer of security.

The New York Times also guards the methodology behind the computation of its best-seller list. *No, it's not just the highest-selling book that makes the cut.*

So what are NDAs?

Non-Disclosure Agreements or NDAs are hugely important in the world of business because they can protect your confidential information being hijacked by employees and other parties. It is a safeguard against disclosing your great business idea and your secret sauce.

These agreements are legally binding contracts between two or more parties where one or more of them agree not to share confidential information with other parties.

How do you use NDAs?

NDAs can be stand-alone agreements or provisions in more complex agreements such as independent contract, advisory agreements or employment agreements.

They may be mutual (both parties agreeing to confidentiality) or unilateral (confidentiality obligations binding the receiver).

Unilateral obligations come in to play when one party shares information about itself or its plans to others such as potential partners, advisers, accountants, investors or lenders.

A mutual NDA is appropriate when there is likely to be an exchange of information between the parties such as in a potential joint venture.

Regardless of your excitement and exuberance about your business plans, irrational or otherwise, exercise the utmost discretion until you have enforceable, well-drafted NDAs in place.

When negotiating an NDA or confidentiality provisions, keep in mind these elements:

As a recipient...

Who is bound and who is liable?

Most people in business do not work alone. Even solopreneurs collaborate with others in producing their products or rendering their services.

As a recipient of confidential information, make sure you are authorized to discuss it with your team. You can agree to and be accountable for the confidentiality obligations being followed by your employees who are bound by confidentiality obligations in their employment contracts.

If you need to discuss this confidential information with third parties such as advisers, make sure you are explicitly permitted to do so and they agree to the same obligations you have been entrusted with.

Be careful before accepting liability for the acts of third parties, however. Unlike your employees, you have little control over your advisers.

Exclusions

There must be appropriate exclusions in place, such as when information becomes public knowledge (through no fault of yours) or when required to disclose information by a court or regulator.

Term

Every good thing must end.

NDAs should have a term during which confidentiality obligations must be maintained.

You and your employees cannot be expected to maintain confidentiality in perpetuity.

As a discloser...

What is "confidential"?

Pay attention to the definition of "confidential information" ensuring that it is specific and includes all information you want protected from exposure.

Key Takeaways

- Exercise discretion when sharing business plans, client data and trade secrets. NDAs protect you but are not bullet-proof
- Ensure NDAs are in place when disclosure of sensitive information is necessary
- Check whether the definition of confidential information is appropriate and covers the information to be disclosed, received or exchanged.
- Check for exclusions, terms and governing law

Jurisdiction - what remedies do you have?

The governing law and jurisdiction of an NDA is also very important.

Remember, generally, mainland courts do not issue injunctions or stay orders.

If an irate employee whose pay increase request you politely declined threatens to spill the beans about your company's repressive work culture, you cannot get a gag order to stop him.

You'll have the option to sue for damages once she's done the deed... unless the NDA is governed by DIFC/ADGM laws and a DIFC/ADGM court issues an injunction.

As you will recall, DIFC/ADGM courts are common-law based courts with injunction issuing powers.

5

Protect Your Chips

"I have two basic rules about winning in trading as well as in life: (1) If you don't bet, you can't win. (2) If you lose all your chips, you can't bet."

- Larry Hite (legendary trader and hedge fund manager)

In October 2019, I attended an intensive equities trading course in Myrtle Beach, South Carolina, run by the wildly successful former US Investing Champion (*yes, there really are investing championships*) Mark Minervini.

I expected the auditorium to be akin to a giant mosh pit full of frenzied, hocked-up stock traders.

Instead, the course kicked off, not with killer strategies on how to make your next million dollars by shorting Tesla but a sedate presentation on risk - the downside.

Before entering a trade, you had to first think of how much you were willing to lose rather than how much you could make.

What?

This seemed counterintuitive for attendees who had coughed up thousands of dollars to learn the skills of making it rain gold.

After all, who wants to talk about losses?

The rationale for a risk-first approach soon became apparent.

Stoicism meets Wallstreet

"The chief task in life is simply this: to identify and separate matters so that I can say clearly to myself which are externals not under my control, and which have to do with the choices I actually control."
— Epictetus, Discourses. 2.5,4-5

One of the essential tenets of Stoicism, an ancient Greek school of philosophy, is the concept of the 'dichotomy of control': understanding what is and what is not within our control and focussing on the former.

Suppose, early one morning, reports of imminent storms and floods flash across your TV screen and mobile phone.

You can either:

a) marshall your resources (something you can control) to get to safety; or
b) look skywards and curse the weather systems (something you cannot control).

According to the Stoics, we have control over ourselves and our actions and these should be the focus of our energies.

You cannot control how much money you will make in stock trading, but you can control how much you will lose.

When entering a trade, it is imperative to know when you will exit if things do not work out as planned.

Every buy order should come with a stop-loss order to automatically sell the stock when it falls to a pre-determined level.

This risk-based approach prevents a slight loss from becoming a massive loss because your loss would be limited to an amount decided beforehand.

You will not lose all your chips.

You will live to fight another day.

This risk mitigation and asset protection approach is critical in business where corporations can shield you from the vagaries of economic forces.

The Sea of Infinite Liability

"Success is not final; failure is not fatal; it is the courage to continue that counts."
- Winston Churchill

Enter the corporation…

Corporations came about in the 1500s to protect investors from the risks of maritime ventures.

At that time, investors organised as partnerships would finance trading ships to venture across oceans.

If the commodity-laden ship made it back in one piece with valuable cargo, the investors would make a windfall.

If the ship was lost at sea or ransacked by pirates, they would be sued in their personal capacity by creditors and face bankruptcy, misery and ruin.

The New World brimmed with new opportunities, yet investors were getting turned off by the inordinate commercial risks.

The Crown was keen to encourage private enterprise and bestowed royal charters upon for-profit ventures engaged in exploration, trade and colonisation - the corporate behemoth that was the British East India Company is a well-known example.

These charters restricted liabilities arising from commercial ventures to the corporations themselves.

Investors would be liable only for their investments and be spared being taken to the cleaners.

If an investor put in 100 pounds toward a ship and it never returned, then the investor would only lose that 100 pounds.

In the words of the inimitable economist, Yanis Varoufakis: *"...for market societies to be able to build hugely expensive things like electricity stations and railways, and for corporations to grow beyond a certain size, the law had to rewritten so that if a business went bankrupt it was only the property belonging to the business that was lost; the personal savings, home, and belonging of the person who ran it were not confiscated."*

The concept of a limited liability company was born.

In the shift from a world of 'societies with markets' to one of 'market societies', CEOs and shareholders replaced Kings and Czars as the "New Rulers of the World" – with corporations at the fulcrum of the changing tide.

Today, as the predominant economic institution of our times, the scale of the modern corporation is staggering in its ubiquity: the clothes you wear, the apples you eat, the phone you use and the bed you sleep on are all produced by corporations.

Today, business failure does need to equate to financial ruin as it did for pre-corporation ship investors of the 1500s.

You can of course do business in several ways.

But doing business without liability protection is like driving a car without brakes.

As an individual, entrepreneur or small business, you want to take advantage of limited liability protection and avoid being adrift on the sea of infinite liability.

So even if your Star Wars-themed sushi restaurant tanks, you may still be able to send your little ones to college.

ENOS

"In the US, the technical term for a limited liability company is a 'corporation', which is ironic because the term derives from 'corpus' ('body' in Latin) – the one thing these corporations lack."

— Yuval Noah Harari, Sapiens: A Brief History of Humankind

As the brilliant author of Sapiens infers, limited liability companies or corporations are deemed a "thing" without actually being a thing. They are entities and exist by themselves.

The term entity comes from the Latin word *enos,* which actually means to be or to exist. While there are differences, the terms corporation, limited liability company or LLC are used interchangeably in this book.

Corporations are distinct, legal entities distinguishable from their owners. The corporate veil of a corporation protects the shareholders of the company from personal liability.

If a customer slips and falls, a temperamental employee punches a pesky supplier, or an employee injures herself on the job, the corporation will be sued and not the owners.

Corporations, therefore, provide personal asset protection and limited liability.

They can protect you from creditors and provide you with a more straightforward mechanism of raising funds, giving you flexibility and management control. They offer estate planning options and privacy of ownership.

Article 71 of the Federal Law No.2 of 2015, Commercial Companies Law ("CCL") in the UAE clearly states that "a partner shall only be liable to the extent of its share in the capital."

As a small business, an LLC structure is essential. It is easy to set up and necessary especially if you deal with the public.

Startups

For startups, an LLC structure provides two additional, critical benefits.

It facilitates the proper issuance of equity to all the founders with a 'vesting schedule' in place.

A vesting schedule (more on this later) contains the carrots the company dangles (like stock options) to incentivise a person to stay on and protect the company if they bail.

Most importantly for startups, LLCs allow for transferring intellectual property, a startup's lifeblood, to the company.

Startups achieve success by bringing innovative ideas to the market and protecting their IP is at the core of their success.

Sole Proprietorships

Sole proprietorships or establishments are cheap to set up and allow you to conduct business anywhere in the UAE, including free zones.

No rules require you to rent office space in a particular area, and you will have no minimum capital requirements.

Sole proprietorships, however, provide no asset protection. The proprietor is in the dock, responsible for every business obligation.

There can also be only one owner of a sole proprietorship. Therefore, it is difficult to sell, and when the grim reaper comes for the sole proprietor, the legal heirs can only sell the business assets and not the business as a going concern.

Partnerships

Whiles general partnerships are easy to establish, you remain liable for your partner's acts.

To adequately protect yourself and your assets, you must incorporate.

You don't want to risk all your chips.

You want to live to invest another day.

The following is a list of business forms available in the UAE:

- Sole proprietorship
- Civil Company
- Limited Liability Company (LLC)
- Partnership
- Private Share Holding Company
- Public Share Holding Company
- Branch of Foreign Companies/Representative Office
- Branch of Gulf Cooperation Council (GCC) company

Startups, LLCs, SMEs and what have you...

The focus of this book is the LLC which is the ideal business form for a new business in the UAE.

SMEs make up 94% of all companies in the UAE, employ 86% of the private sector workforce and generate over 52% of the country's non-oil GDP.

They may be defined as entities engaged in trading, manufacturing or services which meet the thresholds of "employee headcount" and "turnover" and are registered with the DED or with a free zone or industrial zone authority.

While startups are essentially small businesses, it is no longer acceptable to think of them just as smaller versions of large companies.

According to the Silicon Valley icon, Steven Blank, a startup is a "temporary organization designed to search for a repeatable and scalable model," whereas "a company is a permanent organisation designed to execute a repeatable and scalable business model."

Startups and small businesses may both be LLCs.

But there are other notable differences.

A small business such as a nail salon may not be required to be unique, whereas innovativeness were in the DNA of startups such as Airbnb and Uber.

Startups must seek "vertical progress" rather than the "horizontal progress" of small companies.

Peter Thiel gives a good example in his excellent book "Zero to One":

"vertical progress is harder to imagine because it requires doing something nobody else has ever done. If you take one typewriter and build 100, you have made horizontal progress. If you take a typewriter and build a word processor, you have made vertical progress."

The improvement a successful startup offers has to be massive. When it launched in 1995, Amazon "offered at least 10 times as many books as any other bookstore."

These expectations do not hang heavy over the necks of small businesses. A Subway franchise in Jebel Ali or Leicester Square can very profitable without disrupting existing businesses.

Small businesses and startups also differ in terms of their growth and profitability priorities. Startups are expected to grow fast and losses are often overlooked. Amazon, for example, didn't turn a profit for the first nine years of its existence!

When to incorporate?

"The need for change bulldozed a road down the center of my mind."
— Maya Angelou

So you have a great business idea to create, refine or offer a product or service and take it to market.

You even have a shiny, laminated business plan.

So when should you incorporate?

Incorporate when you are ready to move your activity from the realm of a hobby to the world of actual business.

Incorporation is the route to take when you have two or more people working together and entering into contracts with third parties.

While incorporating a company means incurring costs and this may be difficult, especially in the early stages when the finances are tight - it is a proven, reliable mechanism to launch your business while protecting yourself.

Where to register?

The choice of where you register your business can have a far-reaching impact on your business, ability to attract investors and raise funds.

As an individual, entrepreneur or small business, you now have three options of where and how to do your business in the UAE.

You can set up an:

1. Onshore or mainland entity

2. Offshore entity or a

3. Free zone entity

Entity, here, is a generic catch-all term for a business form. Sole proprietorship, partnership and an LLC are all referred to as entities.

Onshore Entities

In 2020, a year of unprecedented changed in the legal landscape of the UAE, the gates to the corporate sector were flung open even further with the removal of the 51% local ownership requirement.

Subject to some exceptions, onshore companies can be wholly owned by non-Emiratis.

A foreign company may also set up in the mainland as a branch. In such a case, the branch would not have a separate legal identity from its parent. It does not require a local partner and the requirement for a local service agent or representative has also been dispensed with.

All legal forms in the UAE mainland are governed by the CCL. The Department of Economic Development (DED) (now known as Dubai Economy) licenses and registers all corporate entities in mainland Dubai.

Offshore Entities

A few free zones such as JAFZA, permit foreign investors to establish offshore companies. They may act as holding companies but are restrained from doing business within the UAE, although they may own property.

Free Zones

Before lifting the local ownership requirements, free zones attracted foreign investments by allowing 100% foreign ownership, unfettered repatriation of funds and exemptions from duties.

The UAE has over 50 free zones, each with its own set of rules and governing authorities. Some are more sophisticated than others.

The nature of your business would affect which free zone you should set up in.

The DIFC and ADGM are financial free zones that encourage investments in banking, finance and Fintech. They have their own regulatory sandboxes and are attractive to tech startups.

The DMCC is a commodities-focused free zone that is rapidly expanding into tech.

If your business depends heavily on imports and exports, it may make sense to locate in a free zone near a port or airport. Jebel Ali Free Zone Authority (JAFZA) and Dubai South have access to the regions largest ports, whereas Dubai International Airport Free Zone Authority caters to the aviation and logistics industry. Commercity caters to the e-commerce industry.

Below is a high level comparison:

	Onshore	Free Zones
Registration authority and approvals	Department of Economic Development (DED)	The relevant Free Zone Authority
Types of legal entities that are permissible	Sole establishment, civil company, branch of a foreign company, LLC, Private/Public joint stock company	Branch of foreign company, single shareholder (FZE), multiple shareholders (FZCO); ADGM and DIFC have their own set of structures which include SPVs and Trusts
Requirement to audit accounts	Yes	Yes
Minimum share capital	In theory, there is no minimum share capital but in practice, it is usually required and varies from Emirate to Emirate	Varies depending on the Free Zone but generally between AED 50,000 to AED 1,000,000
Office requirements	200 square feet minimum	Varies depending on the Free Zone
Markets in which business activity is permissible	No restrictions	Generally only within the Free Zone though there are precedents of FZCOs incorporating branch offices on the mainland and conducting business there

Registering your company

Your company comes into being when you file the required documents with the Department of Economic Development (DED) or the relevant free zone and get issued a trade license.

Numerous corporate services agencies can help you set up your company and they will assist you through the process from end-to-end.

Requirements will vary depending on location and the nature of the business.

Here's a checklist of the steps you will generally need to take are for a mainland license:

- Decide on what kind of business you want to set up
- What do you want to call the business (trade name)?
- Prepare required documents
- Ensure attestation and legalization of required documents with the UAE Embassy in the country of origin
- Apply for initial approval from the DED
- Open a bank account
- Deposit the share capital into the company's bank account
- Obtain office space/flexi desk
- Obtain final approval from the DED
- Obtain trade license
- Register with the Chamber of Commerce

- Register with the Ministry of Labor and Immigration
- Register with the Municipality
- Register with the Civil Defense

Key Takeaways

- An LLC is the most common form of business enterprise in the UAE
- An LLC can protect your assets, grow your business and limit your liability
- Register as an LLC when you are ready to start a business, are working with others and before you enter into contracts
- The best place to register will depend on the nature of your product or service; select an area or free zone appropriate to your business
- To form a company, use a corporate services provider to file the required paperwork with the DED or free zone

Registering your company

Your company comes into being when you file the required documents with the Department of Economic Development (DED) or the relevant free zone and get issued a trade license.

Numerous corporate services agencies can help you set up your company and they will assist you through the process from end-to-end.

Requirements will vary depending on location and the nature of the business.

Here's a checklist of the steps you will generally need to take are for a mainland license:

- Decide on what kind of business you want to set up
- What do you want to call the business (trade name)?
- Prepare required documents
- Ensure attestation and legalization of required documents with the UAE Embassy in the country of origin
- Apply for initial approval from the DED
- Open a bank account
- Deposit the share capital into the company's bank account
- Obtain office space/flexi desk
- Obtain final approval from the DED
- Obtain trade license
- Register with the Chamber of Commerce

- Register with the Ministry of Labor and Immigration
- Register with the Municipality
- Register with the Civil Defense

Key Takeaways

- An LLC is the most common form of business enterprise in the UAE
- An LLC can protect your assets, grow your business and limit your liability
- Register as an LLC when you are ready to start a business, are working with others and before you enter into contracts
- The best place to register will depend on the nature of your product or service; select an area or free zone appropriate to your business
- To form a company, use a corporate services provider to file the required paperwork with the DED or free zone

6

Safeguard your IP

A $157.5 million mistake...

Snapchat's founders Evan Spiegel and Bobby Murphy found themselves in a bind when ousted employee Reggie Brown took legal action against them.

He alleged that he had come up with the idea of the disappearing photo and had not been appropriately compensated when he was booted out of the company.

Snapchat settled out of court for $157.5 million.

Failing to properly transfer the intellectual property had cost the company dearly- a cautionary tale for startups.

Even if you pay a contractor for writing code for you, you don't own the code unless you get whoever wrote the code to sign a document saying that the code was "work for hire".

He clearly didn't just Google that...

Anthony Levandowski was a Google engineer who downloaded company files onto his laptop, exited the building and resigned. He then used the data to establish Otto, a self-driving truck company that was acquired by Uber.

Google filed a case against Uber alleging that Uber was utilising trade secrets stolen by Levandowski to develop its autonomous vehicles.

Within four days of the trial, Uber agreed to a settlement and compensated Google. In a plea deal, Levandowski plead guilty to a criminal charge brought against him for theft of the IP and was fined and sentenced to 18 months.

These two examples showcase the centrality of intellectual property, which is the lifeblood of small companies, especially startups.

"IP" refers to patents, copyrights, trademarks and trade secrets.

Who owns the IP?

As you can see from the Snapchat example, clear ownership and control of IP is a big deal.

Ideally, from a startup founder's perspective, everyone who comes in to contact with your company's valuable IP (such as code) should have signed an NDA and an assignment agreement.

From a startup investor's perspective, things would be different.

If the founders who own the IP have merely licensed (rather than transferred) the IP to the company, then investors may feel like that the founders are hedging their bets. They would want all IP to be vested in the entity and registered (where possible) with the relevant body before handing over cash.

The UAE is a regional leader in the protection and enforcement of IP rights and protecting them here is as important as anywhere else.

Let's take a look at patents, trademarks and copyrights one by one.

Patents

Patent protection is one of the most powerful weapons in the armoury of a small, innovation driven company. It is the shield that little David can use against the behemoth Goliath.

It is a 20-year monopoly over making, using and selling an invention.

In 2015, a jury in Texas awarded a small US company called Smartflash $533 million in damages against Apple for infringement of its patents related to iTunes.

Patents can be monetised and be a recurring source of revenue through royalties/license fees.

Huawei, for example, has a huge catalogue of 5G technology related patents. Despite its mobile phone sales taking a beating, it continues to make about $1 billion annually through royalties related to its patents.

In the UAE, IP may be registered with the Ministry of Economy through the following link: https://u.ae/en/information-and-services/business/intellectual-property

Be careful, though.

Applying for and obtaining a patent can be costly and time-consuming. In a fast-moving market, the patent may be obsolete when the patent is granted so costs must be weighed against potential benefits.

Trademarks

A trademark provides a business with protection over its distinctive name, symbol, catchphrase or tagline. It is a valuable asset of the company, a key component of its brand equity and part of its goodwill, providing it with the legal mechanism to safeguard its gems.

The swoosh and the term "Just do it!" are trademarked by Nike.

You cannot try and sell fake Nike shoes without risking civil and criminal legal action against you.

Register your trademark at https://u.ae/en/information-and-services/business/intellectual-property

Copyright

A copyright is intellectual property protection that gives original, creative works the exclusive right to publish, use, distribute, license, perform and recreate the works.

The good news for creators and authors is that you don't have to register your work. If you created the work, you own it.

As a business owner, however, you may have others create content for your business in art, blogs, graphics, etc.

What happens when your creative sales representative writes a catchy sales blog about the benefits of using your company's AC duct cleaning loyalty program?

You would want such material to be owned by your company as the sales rep is working on your dime.

Here are 3 ways you can ensure copyright ownership:

1. Registration

In the UAE, the work may be copyrighted with the:

i. Copyright Department of the UAE Ministry of Economy
ii. Dubai Copyright Office

The registration process can take up to three months and lasts for the creator's lifetime plus an additional 50 years following the creator's death.

2. A "work for hire" clause or agreement

Work for hire provisions stipulate that work created by employees/independent contractors during their employment shall be automatically owned by the employer (you). This provision relates only to work done during the period they had been employed with you and not to the masterpiece they created the previous year.

3. An assignment agreement

Usually appropriate for one-off arrangements with service providers (designers, photographers, etc.), an assignment agreement transfers ownership of the copyright from one party to another.

Takeaways

- A patent gives you a long-term monopoly over an invention, a trademark will protect your name and logo and copyright will protect your work.
- Ensure work for hire provisions are contained in your contracts with third-party creators.
- Register your intellectual property with the Ministry of Economy.

7

The Benjamins - Raising Funds While Remaining Protected

Armed with a shiny, cutting-edge, business plan about a product that will revolutionise the landscaping industry, you set your eyes on something without which not a leaf will turn: the bankroll, beans, Benjamins, cha-chings, cheddar, dosh or moolah.

You can recheck your bank balance to see if you can cover it yourself, ask your wealthy girlfriend for a loan, approach your friendly banker, attract investors or look for other recent alternatives in the world of raising finance.

Debt capital

When one thinks of taking a loan to start a business (i.e., raising debt capital), it is natural to think of approaching a bank.

But here are some sobering thoughts.

Startups and SMEs make up over 90% of the total number of companies doing business in the UAE.

In Dubai, 95% of all companies, 43% of the workforce and 40% of the GDP are small business-related.

Yet, according to a study, conventional banks in the UAE reject between 50-70% of loan applications submitted by SMEs. As a result, SME lending accounts for only 4% of outstanding bank credit in the country, less than half of the 9.3% of the regional average.

Equity capital

Equity is ownership interest in a company.

Ideally, cofounders should purchase their full equity, or have it allocated to them when the company is formed. This is when the shares are likely to be the cheapest given that the business is just launching.

There are two kinds of stock in the world of startups and SMEs: common stock and preferred stock.

While common stock may be described as plain, regular stock, preferred stock can have additional rights relating to voting, control, and other things.

When you are looking to issue company shares to investors to raise funds (i.e. equity capital) keep in mind that the CCL does not provide for different classes of shares in mainland companies and only the issuance of common stock is possible.

This limitation often makes free zones such as DIFC, ADGM and DMCC the preferred jurisdictions for startups.

Now here are some sources of finance.

Angel Investors

Angel Investors are wealthy individuals, entrepreneurs and families who, as per Forbes magazine, *"invest in early stage or startup companies in exchange for an equity ownership interest."*

Unlike Venture Capitalists, Angel Investors invest their own money.

They assume greater risk compared to banks and Venture Capitalists.

This is one of the quickest ways to get funding as this usually entails minimum paperwork and a more straightforward funding procedure.

If you are looking for angel investors, you can check the website of Dubai Angel Investor (https://www.dubaiangelinvestors.me) and use this as a starting point.

Venture Capitalists

Venture Capitalists (VC) are another potential funding source for your small business.

These are private equity investors who are usually willing to invest large amounts of capital in companies that show potential for rapid growth.

Similar to Angel Investors, VCs rarely require repayment if the business venture fails.

Some of the most active venture capital investors in the UAE include:

- VentureSouq, which invests in high growth early-stage tech companies

    (https://www.venturesouq.com/)

- Shorooq Partners, a leading seed-stage venture capital fund

    (https://shorooq.ae/); and

- BECO Capital, an early-stage venture capital firm (https://becocapital.com/)

Institutions

Getting a loan or an investment from local institutional investors to set up your business is also a viable option.

Institutional investors are companies who have access to other people's funds and invest these into various projects.

Although banks are the most renowned type of institutional investors, other organisations such as insurance companies and mutual funds also provide business funding solutions.

Among the notable institutional investors in the country are Greenstone Equity Partners, the largest fund placement firm in the region, and Gulf Capital, a leading alternative investment company.

Business incubators

Business incubators are organisations that offer full-fledged support to startups, from market positioning and launching to marketing and financing.

Some of the leading business incubators in the UAE are:

- Astrolabs (https://astrolabs.com/)
- Dubai Technology Entrepreneur Centre (DTEC) (https://dtec.ae/)
- In5 (https://infive.ae/)
- FinTech Hive (https://fintechhive.difc.ae/)
- Turn8: (https://turn8.co/about/)
- Techstars Dubai (https://www.techstars.com/)

Governmental Agencies

Set up in 2007, The Khalifa Fund for Enterprise Development seeks to offer support and financing solutions to local investors, entrepreneurs and SMEs in the country: (https://khalifafund.ae/)

Dubai SME, an agency of the Department of Economic Development, is another governmental agency tasked with facilitating the growth of startups and SMEs (https://sme.ae/Default/en)

Crowdfunding

The spread of social media in the 2000s gave birth to a new source of business finance: crowdfunding.

Crowdfunding is a way to raise money from many people to finance projects or businesses.

Crowdfunding has been gaining momentum in the UAE with encouragement from both the Central Bank and the DFSA

The DIFC has crowdfunding regulations in place and has issued licenses to crowdfunding bussinesses such as FundByMe, the Swedish crowdfunding platform.

Takeaways

- While efforts to promote SME lending are in place, it is a small proportion of the overall loan market.
- You can raise finance through debt or equity finance or a combination of the two.
- The shares of a company in the startup and SME world are either ordinary or preferred. Mainland companies can only issue common stock.
- As an entrepreneur, you must consider all financing options available to you. Financing options include family and friends, angel investors, ventures capitalists, institutions, incubators, governmental agencies and crowd funding.

8

Giving Security

"Check yourself, Before you Wreck Yourself."
-Ali G

Cheques

In 2008, Amanda Allen, a UK national, took out a mortgage for AED 2, 380, 000 with Abu Dhabi Commercial Bank. As was customary at the time, she gave the lender an undated cheque for AED 2,337,500.

As the financial crisis worsened, she lost her job, defaulted on the mortgage and left for the UK, leaving over half of her dues unpaid.

The bank called in the loan and processed the cheque, which bounced.

She was prosecuted in absentia, found guilty of dishonestly issuing a cheque contrary to Article 401 (1) of the Federal Penal Code and sentenced to three years imprisonment.

The UAE government sought her extradition under its 2006 extradition treaty with the UK.

While Amanda Allen was not extradited, the case shows the severity with which the dishonouring of cheques has historically been held.

Fortunately, the civil and criminal penalties have been eased since then, with legislative amendments favouring a civil rather than a criminal adjudication of the cheque dishonour.

While issuing a bounced cheque remains a criminal offence, UAE courts have shown increasing leniency over the years. Instead of jail terms, fees and settlements have been the preferred route, especially where the amount is less than AED 200,000.

Regardless, whenever you are asked to submit post-dated cheques - (and you will be when availing a loan or purchasing an asset), remember to "check yourself" and ensure that the cheque is honoured.

Personal Guarantees

Banks in the UAE routinely obtain personal guarantees as security for loans extended to small and medium-sized businesses.

The effect of a personal guarantee is that it makes the guarantor personally liable for the company's debts and essentially removes the limited liability protection an LLC provides.

You and your company become jointly liable, and your obligations become co-extensive.

If your company defaults on loan repayment, the bank may approach a court to have your apartment, car, and favourite painting auctioned and sold. Your bank accounts can be attached.

As an entrepreneur, you will want to avoid issuing personal guarantees. This may prove very difficult to do when seeking a loan from a bank as a small business.

Several factors will affect your negotiations, including the state of your business, the quality of the collateral/security you are able to provide and your relationship with the bank.

Before making a loan to a business, lenders look at credit risk, which is the risk of loss due to a borrower not paying.

Lenders obtain security or collateral to mitigate the risks associated with default.

If you are able to provide alternative security such as by assigning your receivables, mortgaging your assets or creating a charge over one of your bank accounts, then you may be able to avoid signing a personal guarantee.

Travel Bans

Besides homing in on your assets to satisfy their claim, banks can also approach the courts for a travel ban.

A travel ban is an order of court preventing a person from leaving the country.

To obtain a travel ban, a bank must be able to show that a debt exists, the debtor is a foreign national and there are serious grounds to believe that the guarantor is planning to exit the UAE to escape his obligations.

You obviously want to avoid this situation, so be extra careful!

9

Employment & HR

Navigating Non-Competes

A client of mine, a senior executive at an international logistics company based in Dubai, had a Cheshire Cat grin when we met for lunch.

"I've decided the time has come," he said as we sat down. "Fortune favours the brave."

We had not set an agenda for our meeting, so I was intrigued.

"I've decided to take the plunge and set up my own shop," he continued. "I'll need your help with setting up, shareholder's agreements, etc."

Having spent over a decade in the business, he knew procurement and distribution like the back of his hand.

His father had set up a logistics company in his home country. He had lived and breathed the business even before he had started working for this present employer.

When he sent me his employment contract for review, it turned out that he was bound by a pesky non-compete provision. So he was contractually prohibited from opening up his own shop during the one year term of the non-compete provision.

Non-compete agreements prohibit employees from working for a rival business and launching businesses that would compete with the employer's business.

The rationale for these restraints is that an employee should not be free to skip his existing employment armed with client lists, marketing strategies and trade secrets.

That juicy offer of higher pay, a bigger office and double the annual holidays made by a competing business should not be so easy to accept, to the detriment of his employer.

So while non-competes were historically intended to protect trade secrets and proprietary information, they have ensnared schoolteachers, baristas, and janitors in the US.

According to one study, 32% of American companies include them in their employment contracts regardless of the employee's pay or position.

Unsurprisingly, non-compete provisions are a divisive subject.

While the majority of the states in the US allow the enforcement of non-compete provisions, California law outrightly outlaws them. In addition, Washington state makes non-competes unenforceable against certain employees, including those earning less than $100,000 a year.

In the United Kingdom, courts often see non-compete provisions in "restraint of trade" and unenforceable unless reasonable, limited in duration, geographical area, and content. The courts of India and Pakistan take a similar approach.

So too does the UAE.

Article 127 of the UAE Labour Code (Federal Law No. 8/1980) reads:

Should the work entrusted to the worker enable him to meet the clients of the employer or know the business secrets thereof, the employer may require the worker not to compete with him or participate in any competing project upon the termination of the contract. For the validity of such agreement, the worker shall be twenty-one years old at least upon the conclusion thereof, and the agreement shall be limited, regarding time, place and type of work, to the extent for the protection of the legal interests of the employer.

Article (909) of the UAE Civil Code states:

1. *"If a worker, in the course of his work, has access to the secrets of the work or gets acquainted with the customers of the firm, the two*

parties may agree that the worker may not compete with the employer or take part in work competitive to his work after termination of the contract.

2. Nevertheless, such an agreement shall not be valid unless it is restricted to time, place, and type of work, to the extent necessary for the protection of the employer's legitimate interests.

3. It shall not be permissible for the employer to rely on that agreement if he terminates the contract without any act on the part of the worker justifying that course, and likewise, it shall not be permissible for him to rely on the agreement if he commits any act which justifies the worker in terminating the contract."

Article (910) of the Civil Code states:

"If both parties agree that the worker shall be liable for damages if he does not abstain from competition with such liability being unreasonably excessive in order to coerce him to stay with the employer, the condition shall not be valid."

For non-compete provisions to be enforced in the UAE, they must be agreed in writing, limited in time (usually not over 1 year), and specific in the geographic area to which they apply.

Given that mainland courts do not issue injunctions, courts will not restrain the employee from working with a competing business. The employer may file a civil suit for damages against the employee once the employee has begun working at the competitor.

The employer will need to prove direct loss accruing from the employee's breach of the non-compete provisions to succeed. This is challenging as it is often difficult to quantify the loss resulting from a breach of a non-compete provision.

DIFC employment law, a jurisdiction where injunctive relief is generally available, does not address non-compete provisions. However, this does not prevent their inclusion or enforcement.

In 2016, then VP Joe Biden said ""Folks, no one should have to sit on the sidelines because of an unnecessary non-compete agreement." As President he asked the Federal Trade Commission to look into ways to ban or limit their use.

Watch this space.

Employment Contracts

In Mainland UAE, employment contracts may either be limited (or definite) term or unlimited, with the latter being more flexible in scope.

Here are a couple of things to keep in when negotiating them.

Vesting

Vesting refers to the process when an employee is granted a stock option but isn't given the entire amount on the first day.

So, typically an employee will get 25% of their award when she has passed "the cliff" or completed a full year at the company. The rest of their stock will be issued to them in a staggered manner over a period, usually four years.

Vesting is used as an employee retention mechanism.

It can also protect your company if the hiring of that employee doesn't work out as intended. During the four year vesting period, the company can continue to assess whether that employee is worth the equity of the company.

The CCL, which regulates mainland companies does provide for employee share option schemes ("ESOPs") and other long-term incentive plans ("LTIPs"). However, it does not provide for different classes of shares so care must be take when these are contemplated.

Severance

Negotiating severance provisions are as much fun as getting a tetanus shot.

But like the inoculation, negotiating it at the outset can prevent more pain later.

To be entitled to gratuity or severance, an employee is generally required to have worked for one year of continuous service and the dismissal not to be for gross misconduct. An end-of-service gratuity is calculated with reference to the employee's last basic pay at the time of termination.

Takeaways

- Noncompete provisions are permissible under UAE law; to be enforceable, they must be agreed in writing, limited in time (usually not over 1 year), and specific in the geographic area to which they apply.
- Employment contracts may be limited or unlimited
- UAE company law provides for ESOPs, which can be a useful tool to incentivise and retain employees

10

E-commerce

Unless you are amongst the most hardened of Luddites believing, like Newsweek did in 1995, that the internet is just a passing phase, you'll want your business to exist in cyberspace.

No, door-to-door sales are not poised for a splashing comeback.

People spend more time and money online than ever before. Maintaining an online personality is an indispensable element of business.

Whether you sell bicycle pumps, wedding cakes or pet grooming services, it must look impressive in cyberspace.

The UAE's e-commerce sector is also among the fastest-growing in the region and is expected to reach $8 billion by 2025.

Amazon's $650 million USD acquisition of Souq.com in 2017 was early confirmation of the region's burgeoning ecommerce growth and potential.

While Amazon and Noon.com continue to battle it out for online dominance, several online platforms such as Sellship.co and tradeling.com offer online, integrated services to small businesses.

Like setting up a bricks-and-mortar gig, establishing an online business in mainland UAE requires an application to the DED for issuing an online business trade license. This application then requires the approval of the telecommunications regulator, the Telecommunications Regulatory Authority.

If your entire business is online-retail-focused, you could consider registering your company in Dubai Commercity (https://www.dubaicommercity.ae/).

It is a free zone dedicated to supporting the growth of the eCommerce market in the Middle East and North Africa (MENA) region and has a readymade ecosystem for online businesses.

Here are four ways to protect your business online.

1. **Grab your domain name**. Check the major internet registries such as GoDaddy, Netregistry and Bluehost to see if your preferred name is available. If it is, register the .com and .ae domains together with any other ones that may have a nexus. You want to avoid the risk of having to deal with annoying cybersquatters who register domains with

your trade name and then try to extort money from you for it. The risk of this increases as your business grows.

2. **Create Contractual Protections**: Electronic contracts are enforceable in the UAE and your website should contain appropriately drafted terms and conditions, contracts, disclaimers and a privacy policy.

3. **Ensure Local Compliance:** Be sure that your online presence complies with local laws and regulations. For example, if you are an online business, ensure you have a valid online business license issued the DED in your emirate and comply with its terms.

4. **Become GDPR Compliant:** As a UAE-based business, you must not only comply with local laws but also seek to be GDPR-compliant, especially if you are looking to do business in the EU and the US.

What the heck is GDPR?

General Data Protection Regulation (GDPR) is a set of regulations to protect consumer data. The intention behind it is to return to EU citizens, full control of their personal data such as email addresses, social networking posts and their IP information. If you process or hold information relating to EU citizens, you will be subject to the GDPR.

Therefore, you will want to ensure compliance to avoid a hefty EU fine.

11

Consumer Protection

As a supplier of goods and services, you will want to comply with the Consumer Protection Law (Federal Law No, 15 of 2020) or "CPL". Breaching it can lead to imprisonment and fines.

As a consumer, you will want to know your rights, know when you are being scammed and what you can do about it.

The CPL applies to all goods and services within the UAE, including in free zones and includes e-commerce transactions if the supplier is registered in the UAE.

It introduces a consumer's right to privacy and bans the use of the customer's personal data for promotion and marketing purposes.

Although other languages may be used, businesses must provide their marketing material, terms of service, the privacy policies in Arabic.

E-commerce businesses also cannot don a cloak of invisibility and exist only in cyberspace: names, legal status, address, details of licensing authority, products, payment and warranties must be provided.

Under the CPL, consumers have the right to:

1. have increased awareness of their rights and obligations
2. a "fair and quick settlement" of their disputes
3. "fair compensation" for the damage caused to them or their property because of purchasing or using the goods or receiving the services provided by suppliers
4. repair, maintenance, or after-sales services, or the return, replacement, or reimbursement of the product

The penalties for violating certain provisions of the CPL, such as false advertising, can lead to imprisonment of up to two years and a fine up to AED 2 million.

12

Time to turn off the lights?

Bankruptcy

What happens when things don't go as planned and angry lenders bang on your office door?

Before you throw in the towel and go back to your old job as a claims adjustor, there are a few issues you must address.

Reorganization

Some countries extend protections to companies unable to pay their debts.

Under a Chapter 11 bankruptcy in the United States, courts can appoint a trustee and task them with reorganizing a company's dues to revive the company's financial health. During this process, the company can continue business with some protection from creditors and have a shot at re-emerging as a viable business.

Hertz's car rental business was badly hit by the COVID-19 pandemic and the company was forced to enter in to

Chapter 11 bankruptcy. However, as I write this, it is emerging with a reorganization plan that has investors excited about its prospects. Yesterday, its stock price rose 63%.

While several jurisdictions follow these reorganization principles, the UAE bankruptcy regime does not have a chapter 11 corollary.

Until 2016, the UAE lacked a single, cohesive insolvency regime.

Following the financial crisis of 2008-2009, UAE bankruptcy processes came under greater scrutiny and were increasingly seen as archaic. Of particular concern was that there was no single source of law governing bankruptcy procedures and the mechanism was an amalgam of disparate parts.

The calls for reform grew louder.

In 2016, the UAE Bankruptcy Law came into force and streamlined bankruptcy procedures applicable to onshore companies.

Two procedures emerged:

1. Protective Composition; and

2. Formal Bankruptcy which can either be a rescue process similar to Protective Composition or liquidation (sale of company assets to pay its debts)

Protective Composition

Based on the French *sauvegarde* model (which means 'protection' in French) Protective Composition gives ailing companies a chance to dream of better days.

If you have not defaulted on your dues to your lenders for over 30 days and those holding two-thirds of your outstanding debts, agree, you can apply to the court for Protective Composition.

If approved, all court proceedings are suspended and a court-appointed trustee then negotiates a rescheduling and repayment plan. Unlike in the US and the UK, there are no "cram-down" provisions whereby the bankruptcy reorganization is imposed by court order despite objections by certain classes of creditors.

For this to work, you would need empathetic lenders who believe that your business's revival is not a mere pipe dream.

In my experience, most lenders in the UAE prefer to enter into a re-financing of existing loans - extension of repayment periods and/or enhancements in facility amounts

Formal Bankruptcy

As a debtor, you or your creditors may apply for a formal bankruptcy where a court-appointed expert assesses your company's financial condition and whether the bankruptcy criteria has been met.

If the application is accepted, unsecured lenders are prevented from taking further action and must evidence their claims.

An important aspect to remember is that the bankruptcy process does not bind secured creditors (lenders holding collateral) who can go after their piece of the pie regardless of the proceedings but with court permission.

The court orders the preparation of a report on whether restructuring is viable and this is then considered by the courts and the creditors.

If they consider the prospect of revival favourably then the principles of Protective Composition largely apply.

If no light is seen at the end of the tunnel and lenders holding two-thirds of the debt agree, a formal liquidation is ordered. The company's assets are sold to pay the debts and you shut the lights off on the way out of the office.

Protecting yourself from personal liability

Transactions that occurred within a two-year period prior to initiation of insolvency proceedings may be scrutinized by the court. In addition, there is a risk of directors being held personally liable, so obtaining sound legal advice early on is critical.

Emergency provisions

A new chapter 15 was added to the Bankruptcy Law to protect companies during an Emergency Financial Crisis.

An Emergency Financial Crisis is defined as "a general situation that affects trade or investment in the country, such as a pandemic, natural or environmental disaster, war, etc."

Personal Insolvency

The UAE now has a Personal Insolvency law which applies to individuals facing financial difficulties.

It is a court-led process and that offers the possibility of a settlement plan to a natural person who is unable to meet his or her financial obligations.

You can check your personal credit score by downloading the Al Etihad Credit Bureau app and entering the required information.

You can download it here:

https://apps.apple.com/ae/app/aecb-creditreport/id1375991737

Key Takeaways

- The Bankruptcy Law of 2016 governs corporate bankruptcies relating to mainland companies in the UAE. It provides mechanisms for Protective Composition and Formal Bankruptcy for businesses unable to meet their liabilities.
- Unlike the US and the UK, UAE Bankruptcy Laws do not contain "cram-down" provisions and do not generally bind secured creditors.
- A personal bankruptcy regime also exists. It applies to individuals facing financial difficulties and offers various settlement options if the case fulfils specific criteria.

Epilogue

Congratulations, you've made it!

We just covered nine aspects of doing business in the UAE.

It was a brief walk through the country's business environment.

Along the way, we discussed ways to protect your assets, guard your information and protect your interests.

You have seen the utility of limited liability companies and how they can be a bulwark against the uncertainties of the marketplace while launching your businesses.

You have seen ways to protect your intellectual property, safeguard your rights and how to thrive in one of the most vibrant economies in the world.

Before you go

Thank You!

I want to thank you for purchasing this book.

I hope you found it helpful, and I wish you the best of luck with your ventures.

I'd like to ask you for a small favour.

If you enjoyed the book, I'd be very grateful if you could leave an honest review on Amazon (I read them all).

Every single review counts, and your support does make a difference.

So…

Scan this QR code or Click Here https://tinyurl.com/hrwv9ph4

On the off chance, if you really didn't like my book, could you contact me with your thoughts? I would love to hear your criticism.

Thanks again for your support!

To your success!

Kamal

If you have any comments or questions, please reach me at info@kamaljabbar.com

Further information available at: www.kamaljabbar.com

LinkedIn   Instagram   Facebook   Twitter

ACKNOWLEDGMENTS

I want to thank:

- my father Javed Jabbar, whose persistent exhortations to "keep writing" may finally be bearing fruit
- my mother Shabnam and sister Mehreen for righting the ship whenever it veered off course
- Zainab for being a super-mom to our little cherub
- Ziyad Hadi for his prompt, incisive comments on the first draft of the manuscript.
- Mumtaz Mustafa (@mumtazmustafadesigns) for being a long-standing, (long-suffering) unpaid consultant in all matters design
- Ziad Zafar for keeping the laughter factory running and for regular doses of much needed absurdity
- Wim Hof and his method, for keeping the mind limber

Printed in Great Britain
by Amazon